Difficult Chickens

COLORING BOOK

Illustrated by Sarah Rosedahl

ISBN-13: 978-0692601945 (Tolba Farm Press)
ISBN-10: 0692601945

www.srosedahl.com

Ameraucana

Brahma

Derbyshire Redcap

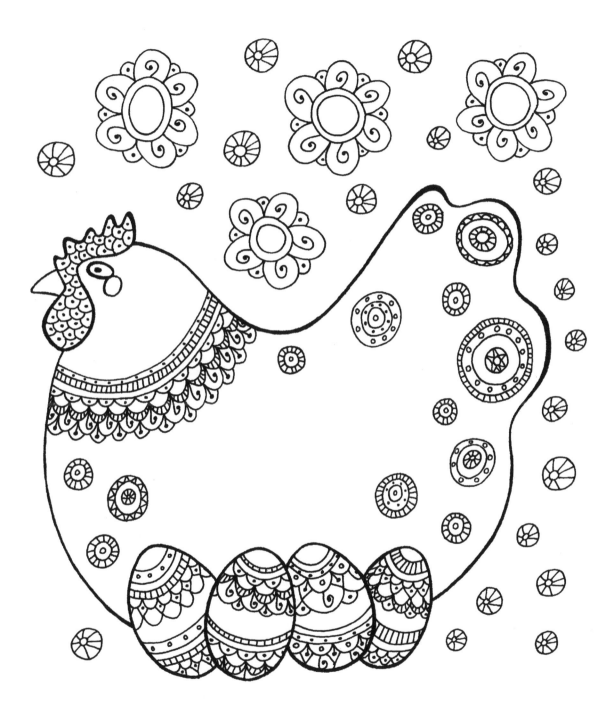

Easter Egger

Faverolles

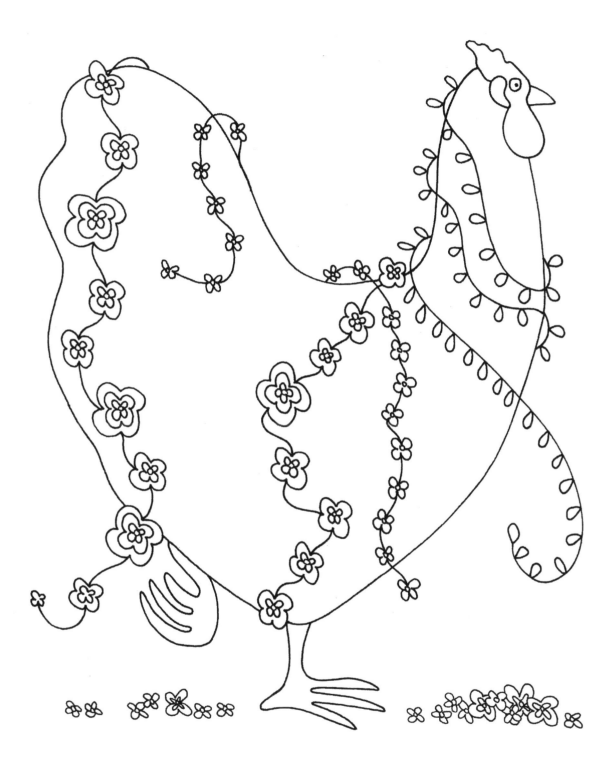

Hamburg

Iowa Blue

Jersey Giant

K osovo Long Crowing Rooster

Leghorn

New Hampshire Red

Rosecomb

Silkie

Wyandotte

Yokohama

Made in the USA
Lexington, KY
10 December 2016